Fortress of the Muslim

PROPHETIC INVOCATIONS
FROM THE QURAN & SUNNAH

Fortress of the Muslim

PROPHETIC INVOCATIONS
FROM THE QURAN & SUNNAH

Sa'id bin Ali bin Wahf Al-Qahtani

1 2 3 4 5 6 7 8 9 10

All rights reserved. No part of this publication may be reproduced, stored in a retrieval system or transmitted in any form or by any means – electronic, mechanical, photocopying, recording or otherwise – without written permission from the publisher.

© Light Publishing 2014

Sa'id bin Ali bin Wahf Al-Qahtani

Fortress of the Muslim
Prophetic invocations from the
Quran and Sunnah

ISBN 978-1-915570-00-0

www.lightpublishing.co.uk

CONTENTS

Selected Inspirational Poetry   1

Part I
PROCESS
Long Light   7
Then   9
The Only Way   13
Extinction Rebellion?   15
Keepers I   19
Keepers II   21
Followings   23
Cairn   25
Creative Rest   27
Your Story   31
The Creative Way   35
Placenta   37

Part II
PRODUCE
Rising   41
Creating   43
Go There   45
Fire   47
Be the Water   51
Helpless to Help   53

Flow	55
Children of the Sun and Moon	57
Breakthrough	59
How You See	61
Whatever	63

Part III
PURPOSE

The Calling	67
The Writer's Call	69
Truth To Tell	71
A Reply And An Answer	75
Halo	77
These Times	79
Human Being	81
I Am	83
Let's Keep in Touch	85
Award Winning Inspirational Poetry	87
Acknowledgments	91
About The Poet	93

SELECTED INSPIRATIONAL POETRY

READING MOTIVATIONAL POETRY

This is a book of motivational poetry, that aims to induce motivation through connecting with and releasing your creative energy.

Not energy of the rip-roaring, *rah-rah-rah* kind that tends to fire and then falter but the energy that consistently flows through you and through everything. The flow has carried you from childhood to wherever you are right now, reading this. The flow that is always there in you, like the water table beneath the ground, but sometimes not accessible though the dust and dirt and debris of everyday life.

When you immerse yourself in this flow, life makes sense and everything becomes easy. These poems aim to ease you in.

Some encourage you to do (and be) what you love. Some encourage you towards your own definition of greatness. Some aim to pick you up when you fall or the going gets rough. Some let you know that you can make it. Some invigorate and vitalise.

INSTRUCTIONS FOR READING MOTIVATIONAL POETRY

- Find a place where you won't be disturbed for a little while and sit in a comfortable way. Add cushions, blankets, candles, anything that makes you feel more easeful and comfortable.
- Take a deep breath, sigh heavily on your out breath, then consciously relax.
- Connect to the fact that you are breathing. Don't change your breath just yet. Just observe it. Stay connected, brain to breath, for a few moments.
- If your mind is very busy, try this: On your next out-breath, breathe all the way to the end. When you reach the end, breathe out further. Engage your chest muscles to help you squeeze out more air. Then relax.

Observe your in-breath happening by itself. See how it rushes in, spontaneously, without effort. That is creative response that poetry can produce. Repeat two more times.
- Now open a page, and read your chosen poem silently or aloud.
- Notice if your mind wanders, gently bring it back to the words on the page. Give them your full attention while you're there.
- When you're finished the poem, sit still. Don't move away. Don't rush to read another one. Don't analyse. Don't judge. Just let it reverberate, like the sounding of a bell, within you.
- Connect to your breath again.
- Read the poem again.

MORE POETRY

A motivational poem read well dissolves confusion and fosters clarity, dissolves anxiety and cultivates peace, dissolves distraction and focuses flow. It provides a refuge within which to recharge and reconnect with the truth of life.

I hope that you'll enjoy these poems. Read them aloud, copy lines into your f-r-e-e-writing notebook or journal, pass them onto your friends. This, to me, is the highest praise, dearer than any prestigious award.

Until next time, may your life be filled with poetry!

x Orna

PS: If you like the poems in this book, you can support my work, and receive an exclusive little poetry book from me monthly, by signing up as a patron at OrnaRoss.com/poetry-patrons (just £2.50 a month)

PART I
PROCESS

LONG LIGHT

Every light creates a shadow, the stars
can't shine without the night. Seek to muffle
up your sorrow: feel life fade inside,
and out. Loose it. Let it sear you hollow,
slice you open, clear your throat. Long
light lives through grace of shadow. The
    stars
are pleased to shine through night.

THEN

Then, one October evening,
as dusk was coming in
like a train running
too fast on its tracks,
in the kitchen corner finding
the hushed breath of you,
sleepy but awakening,
in the heat of our house.
Butterfly.

Up you rose, to circle
around me once,
then twice, enmeshing me
within the old sayings and stories,
from the first home.
Dealan dhé.

"May the wings of the butterfly
that kissed the sun,
light on your shoulder
in the heart of your home."

"A butterfly in the house,
is the light of a soul crossing,
the brightness of the Gods,
the burning stick shaken
to create the need-fire."

The need-fire. Flame attained
by friction, the rubbing of sticks.
Then neighbours for miles around
attending with their beasts.
Cattle and horses and swine
passing through the fire
and its smoke
in order of age and dignity,
in all solemnity.
Then home,
and the hearth fires relit
each householder rekindling
from the one, central fire.

The souls of the dead are always crossing.
Knowing it's too cold outside for you, now,
too warm within for hibernation,
I find a cool place for you to winter.

Taking you there, carrying your frail dreams
with care in a two-handed hold,
wondering. What is the meaning of this?
What might be about to transform?

THE ONLY WAY

Though
it feels like we're
on our way
somewhere,
we're only ever here,

forever

ending
where we begin,
spiralling
infinitesimal
instants.

So
when we feel

we've been.

stopped.

in our tracks
it's really life
calling us away
from peril and sin

saying: "Come now.
dear one. What's in
your way is your way."
Time to face in.

EXTINCTION REBELLION?

I see the sun rise in the east,
over the waves, and am brought
to wonder at its endeavor.
Do you think we'll ever know
what we should do with human trying?
How to forgive the plying of fear into flags
how to caress the fists of effort, open
them out and kiss the wrinkled palms
for needing too hard, for calling war?
How we might quiver into feeling
the rest of our being?

The neck as honored to lower as to lift.
The back made to bend or return to erect.
The arms that can splay as well as hug close.
The chest with its close encasement of ribs,

so open between and behind,
holding, without touching,
the lungs it exists to protect.
The diaphragm allowing the softness
of breath. The stomach digesting,
removing the waste. The pelvis,
its bowlful of organs and needs. The legs
that can run and fall to their knees.
The feet that can stop as sure as they stalk.
And the hands. Those twin beings
outgrowths of our wrists,
that can interlace fingers,
or spiral and twist,
cup fistfuls of air to throw over hair
to fall flowing,
or splash into a face
that knows how to smile,
into eyes that can own what they own,
into ears that can hear cries harmonizing
across tongues that tell longing in song,
along trunks that undulate dance out of
    howls,
through a being that knows how to belong.

I see the sun in the west, over land
receding, revealing all the other bodies
of light and wonder at that revelation.
Do you think we'll ever allow
moon and stars to lead us

into the kindness of dark?
Let the flags of the nations wave
gaily, without flapping the skin
and skulls of our sons? Know
the he-men who unpin the bombs
are also she-girls in the dark,
ashamed of their need,
calling for mommy through dreams
of delivering imperfect ribbons of peace.

With each of us a devil divine
do you think we will ever call time
know which parts we must hold
with rejoicing,
which must be let go?
And how?
Bury our weapons
so deep they can't be recalled
except as low warning
of death ways long gone?
Hold gently the creatures
of the depths and the shores
and let them lead us
out of our charge towards the end
into what we could—still yet—become,
if we could only know how,
if we could but unfurl to allow?

KEEPERS I

Up beside yon ancient castle
Where a knight stands in the hall,
Crumbling bricks square off a garden,
Broken chapel, under pall.

Crooked graves lie mossed with lichen,
Twisted bramble gates the we all,
While the knight, once thought
A warden, arbor empty, holds the hall.

KEEPERS II

I'm taking out the trash,
throwing away old notes,
worn thoughts and images.

A woman's bare back
a little scratched,
half-broken. A man
with an eagle on his hand
a belly full of complaint.

An empty house
on an abandoned island,
darkening down.

Unremarkable repeats.
I won't create anything

like that again.

Now I want to go where
a woman is old enough
to have the head
of a lioness,
where a man knows
how to be his own cub.
Where two beings—
neither fish nor fowl—
can swim together
in or out of the tide,
beyond the weir,
buoyed by the swell.

It has taken me time
to learn to see like this.

The repeats whisper
their notes on their way
to the trash.

I will keep
this poem.

FOLLOWINGS

Creatives grope through the dark
drawn by the promise of dawn
our way lit by the stars
who smile on our stumbles
know why we seek
and love what our searching creates.

CAIRN

On the beach,
a dozen stones,
prone and stacked,
one atop another
held in place
by the time and care
it takes
to harness the force of gravity
and hold it all together
in the fine balance
of challenge, chance, and choice.

CREATIVE REST

Now is your time
to pull in and go slow.
Take shelter
from the fumigating
ways of the world.

Your skin is grey,
your powder is dry.
Soft words are blasphemies,
pieties binding your nerves
in corsets of thought.

The air tastes of smoke.
The air tastes of fumes.
There is nothing
to fear, yet here it comes

in waves. Afraid, afraid.

Come to center.
You've known days of reaching out
to the burdened beside you. Stay giving,
but this time, give to yourself.
Find a space you can live in.
safe to breathe, and keep breathing.

For now, lose what's left of the light.
Darkness is a place to gather what's sacred,
to burn incense till dawn. Feel how it feels
to slip free of your whalebones
and tenterhooks, to trust
in the power of the pause.
Lie here and ask for your needs.
We'll bring you water, a blanket, a kiss.

The body pulses with the tides.
Let yourself fall and then
rise.
Let time ride and come round,
in its time. When sky opens beyond
the window you'll thrill to alight
on the breeze and disperse.
But not now. No. Now
is your time to pull in
and go slow.

YOUR STORY

I
A curve in the road.
Fog coming down.
All you can see ahead
is the face of a hedge
and at your feet, a ditch.
This, after that hill
that was nothing but up,
and up and up, for miles,
and that left you, last evening,
in the dusk, with the road
all but falling away,
one foot dangling in mid-air,
dark swirling.
Knots in your insides
today, as you recall it.

A close thing is a close thing.

II
And now: this blurred outcrop
of foliage and furrow,
cutting you off, sight unseen,
in this lonely outpost,
in these boots,
leaning on this staff,
unable to step forward.
You turn that corner.
Get beyond one curve,
and another swerves up.
And up. You can't go on.
You must go on.

III
And then, in one instant,
landscape opens out
and reveals itself.
A carpet of hillside and field.
In the distance, the town,
nestled in its valley,
two church spires,
a jigsaw of houses
and shops clustered by the sea.
And the road that brought
you here. Ha! That road.
It made you fit and strong

enough to climb its twists
and turns, by twisting
and turning you as it took you
up and up, to this height here,
where all the routes—the streets
and lanes and byways—
can be seen.

And it will carry you back, now,
to where you need to go,
deliver you down, with ease,
into what lies ahead.

THE CREATIVE WAY

Across the sea
of your imagination
lies that fertile land
you want to reach.

Though the way
from here to there
is barely visible
and seems impossible,
you've come so far.

Fix your eyes
on the island
of your dream
and take the next step
you need to take

to reach it.
Feel the sands slip
beneath your feet,
the waters rise,
the tidal tug,
and know:
what's in your way
is your way.

And though it's good
to have an end
in mind, in the end
what matters most
is how you go.

PLACENTA

Look to the tree, how it remembers the clay
    that once pressed,
loam-loving, round its kernel; through which
    it roamed out, a tender
and unseeing shoot, groping towards the
    light of day and the airy,
spangled light of night; poked itself up, thin
    and twiggy-green, dazzled

and drawn by the taste of wind, the touch of
    sky, to rise and rise.
Oh yes, sap soaring, up it flew, thickening to
    wood as it went, circling
its circles, and pouring out leaves and fruit,
    leaves and fruit, leaves and fruit,

to flare and fall, year after year, from its
    trunk. One dear trunk, so

tall and split and spread, fingering the air, its
    strength its equal, rooting reach for earth.

PART II
PRODUCE

RISING

You can be killed off
for a time.
You may need to rest,
retreat, reverse,
repair a wing.

But keep the faith.
Hold true.
Trust in your desire to do
the thing you want to do.

Come the given day,
out of buried time
you'll unearth
some new devising.

You'll know just how
to step forth again,
and soar into your rising.

CREATING

Through the furnishings
of your house,
the sweat
of your work,
the whorls
of your fingerprints,
your longing,
and that of your ancestors', glows.

No, flesh is not the final word.
To be human is to be a ghost
for most of eternity. A trail
of doing and destroying.
Before and after, a shade,
an echo of air, through ice crystals,
dust particles, asteroids.

Meantime,
you are here, reading.
Feeling and thinking.
And electrons dance to your tune.

Throughout the cosmos
the great fire is blazing
in the great calm,
as wonders
await your wanting,
seeking the channel of your desire,
so they can be born.

GO THERE

When hurt and sorrow rise
and the news of the day inveigles
with its scandalised dispairs,
I retreat to my lair,

where the tall trees
sway in waiting for me,
brushing the sky
with their leaves;

where the stream breaks
over the stones,
knowing how to flow
without straining
forward in fear;

where above me,
secret stars,
veiled in the light of day,
know just how much
we need nighttime to see.

There, in the greening
spirit of trees,
under the blue dream
dome of the sky,
by the winged babble
of water, I hear myself
sigh, fall into grace,
and fly free.

FIRE

To hold a flame,
you must already burn.
And you do,
with a dragon's fire roar,
louder than a thousand jet engines
taking off, flaring to stain
the sky blood red
copper bright,
melting gold.

Your fire keeps you
throwing yourself at the door
of your own sky. You won't stop
until you answer yourself,
allow your own lighting.
If you stay closed

you will still kindle
within and without, burning
down your barricades.

So succumb. Let it win.
Be sucked in
to the violet-blue heart
at its root, flicker back out
in yellow tongues to lick
aura and skin and blood

Aureate air.
Fiery flesh.
Liquid brass.

And then, when
you're gone, you
will ignite you again.
Fire yourself back
into the infinite
life that is of you
and not you,
the eternal blaze
consuming everything
but itself.

You hold the flame
Already, you burn.

BE THE WATER

Be the water.

As in the river
carving itself
and its boundaries
with its own body.
Its soft power
seeing stone yield,
mountain crumble,
and majesty revealed.

Be the water.

As in the pool
where a dropped stone
sees semi-circles ripple,

visible and submerged
for measures beyond
generating all kinds
of differences.

Be the water.

As in the ocean
wave bellies swelling and falling,
to break and retreat.
to swell again, and repeat,
and underneath, holding
still fathoms deep.

Be the water.

HELPLESS TO HELP

Again, another season of pain.
We watch, helpless to help
as you're taken,
thrust back to the time
when the scourge
was planted, brought
to blood in the place
you thought you'd vacated.

Yes, it is safe to dissolve.
Yes, memory must mourn,
but don't linger too long
in hesitation, transfixed
by yesterday's thorns.

May your tears fall

in a way that sates
your thirst for the wounding.

Remember your future
the land of your dreams.

Life is dreams come true
or dreams outworn.
In the matter of dreams, it seems,
there are no in-betweens.

Led by pain,
a better way awakens.
Led by longing,
sweet mystery unfolds.

FLOW

I wish we could flow as oceans tide,
swelling with joy at our pulse to unfurl.

I feel we should roll as planets turn,
dark days and seasons held level with light.

I sense we can grow as mountains rise
from stresses rock setting, solid and free.

I intend to go as children run,
arms wide, smile plunging, into full stop.

CHILDREN OF THE SUN
AND MOON

When you need
you can always summon up
the dormant infants in yourself
the two you used to be
before sex segregation
girl and boy.

Gather them each
into your arms. Allow your eyes
to brighten in the light
of theirs, sun and moon,
and let them look at you,
until you see.

Then smiling,
set them down again,

these twin orbs of you,
give each one of your hands
and let them lead you back,
so you can proceed
the way you came.

BREAKTHROUGH

Whenever you're feeling stopped,
as if you're locked
within a skin of glass,
held back from where
you long to go,
it's time to consciously
breathe in,
to turn attention
from the outer ways,
and take some space to play.

Investigate the inner glaze,
what it keeps safe.
Explore the self it holds in place,
now on the brink of change.
Illuminate creative spirit's

love for you.
Support its drive
towards what you want to do.
Then let it be. Step back and wait.

Beneath our glass-eyed wont
to ruminate,
breakthrough rotates.
With rest and play,
it swells in place,
breathes out,
and snaps its straits.

HOW YOU SEE

Born into being
from the constellation of thoughts
and responses within,
and the distant-down depths
of all we've been given:
our sense of seeing.

No one else sees how
you see.

Let us look.
Stop our incessant blinking.
Sink into each flicker of rest.
Draw down our lids
and return
to the cosmos within.

Lenses rinsed clear
of the world's debris
open up. Invite in the gods
to gaze through our eyes.
What arrives into sight
is borne on our being.

No one else sees what
you see.

WHATEVER

FOR ORNAGH

Whatever you do,
my dear maker,
don't go looking for yourself,
or seeking to improve.
You are not to be *found*,
and nothing whatever in you
needs to be *fixed*.
You, my beauty, are
what you are
and whatever you are
currently
creating from that.

You don't need
to be political,
or emblematical.

Charitable
or intellectual.
You have no need to repent.

The motion you seek is release.
Relent. And whatever you make
from the undulating being
you've been given,
make it loud.
Do it proud.

PART III
PURPOSE

THE CALLING

I have come to you now.
Open your ears
the pores of your skin
the blades of your back.
Unself yourself.

I have come
because I know you
and it is time.

Let go of your pathways.
I have brought you thus far.
I do not want to abandon you
on the road.

Listen. My sound is like

the praise prayer of a lover.

Its pulse is calling you up
through the underbelly swell of the tide
the hidden side of the clouds
the wing face of the wind.
It can raise you above the moon.

Yes, I am asking you to fly.
Have I not given you the skies?

THE WRITER'S CALL

Your words must scrub the floor for love,
I heard it all declare. I kissed my pen,
swore this decree to air.
Then set to work on bended knee, a childlike
    creep
through house and street, to clean through
what's encrusted there.

It's done for you, kind reader, dear,
who walks my words across the page,
who seeks clear ground in marks I make:
that glisten in your gleaning eye,
that shines with mine, us both to see
how in the clearing, all can be.

TRUTH TO TELL

Morning, May in England, Ascot Priory
   wood.
In a clearing by the pathway, a branch
invites a bow. I lay my forehead
on its bark, its skin
on mine is cool with rain.

These trees once belonged to nuns
who too found time, between
bell and candle, to walk and wonder,
to look overhead when summoned
by the wind's reason and the leaves' reply.
Now that whisper is for me and my friends,
here for a retreat.

My room in this place once was someone's

home. I see her rise again, step into her stiff
black habit, hide her hair. At the corner sink,
a splash, one brisk eye to the mirror. Soft
shoes shuffling out, along corridor tiles
to Mass. Head bowed to altar,
her day an offering to the glory of her God,
His greater good.

Safe, safe within her solid priory walls,
how could she ever have imagined
a few decades on her room for hire?
And to the likes of me and my friends?
And all her sisters, and all their way of life,
all gone? In the graveyard underneath
the trees they lie coffined, row on row.
Each has a wooden cross to tell:
her name; her age at death;
how many years she lived 'in religion'.

Above them a giant Jesus still presides,
all iconography intact: spike nailing
feet, one above the other, to the wood;
cloth closed round the primal place,
protected even in last agony. Open chest
and arms and palms; crown of thorns;
and, of course, the beard. This God's
a man, make no mistake.

Oh, what a tale to tell.

I grew up in grounds like these
with nuns who tried to teach His way
with sticks and prayers. 'Thou
Shalt Nots' ruled their days
and ours and almost always failed us.
But still. Still the story stands,

on more than rod, or rule, or cross,
passing on the all that whispers always:
wind to leaf, sap to skin,
ever on and back again,
so that tonight, I'll lie down
in my nun's room, imagining
her way, knowing how
it came to end
is how mine must begin.

A REPLY AND AN ANSWER

I.
Listen, my parents,
the grasses are crawling,
the trees are thrumming,
soon birds won't be able to sing.
Listen. Hear me.
Our time is for turning.
If the old ways don't die, we
can't win.

II.
Listen, my children: the grasses are
crawling, the trees are
thrumming, birds know what they know
as they sing.

Listen... Hear it.
True time ever calling.
Lay down your despairing,
join in.

HALO

My brother, Conor, used them as they should
    be used,
the rings. Hoops of grey rubber to throw at
    numbered
hooks on a board and make the grown-ups
    who came

to our bar for their daily drink call out. *Well
    done!*
To me they were things to twirl atop my
    four-year-old
pointy fingers, till they flew. Or to array my
    arms,

making of me a Sheba or a Cleopatra, queen
    of places

with names like Abyssinia or Timbucktoo. Their
circle of air was a space, pregnant with everything.

And the black board where you were supposed to chalk
the tally was where, up on a barstool, I liked to practice
writing: A. And B. And C. And where, one day, I was caught

by a moment I now know will hold me rapt through
all eternity: when meaning came swimming towards
me, in white out of black, and set me smiling: Apple!

And Ball! And Cat! Behind, Conor threw a ring and men
were calling. *Yes! Score! Good man yourself!* while I cast
off, and lay down in language, braceletted wrists aloft.

THESE TIMES

"This too will pass,"
the ancients said
and so it did
but so too did it stay
within the human race
in memories
if not in ways.

And so we've come to here,
this surface blur called now,
its depths though
a clear echo.

Listen. Hear.

Earth still holds out her arms

as she sends up
her wake-up calls.
She knows.

And we born of the earth,
her seas and stars,
know too.
Can we bear to plunge
into the wound and find
the pearl
the question passed to us.
What can we make
and mend
to make amends?

We have, now, what we need
and the whole world
has shown, now, how
it can act as one.
The time is come.

HUMAN BEING

You were born
with a mouth.
A tongue, two lips,
and twice times two lines
of teeth were given,
the first in year two,
then at seven.
All thought through,
what you'd need
to savour and speak,
to kiss and to coo.
So please: do.

I AM

I have thoughts
but I am not my thoughts. I am
the one who sees them swirl.
What can be seen is not
the seer.
I have thoughts but my thoughts are not me.

I have a body
but I am not my body. I am
the one who makes it move.
What can be moved is not the mover.
I have a body but my body is not me.

I have feelings
but I am not my feelings. I am
the one who feels them feel.

What can be felt is not the feeler.
I have feelings but my feelings are not me.

I have wants
but I am not my wants. I am
the one who knows desire.
What can be known is not the knower.
I have wants but my wants are not me.

LET'S KEEP IN TOUCH

Enjoyed the poems? Would you like more? If you're online, we have lots of ways to continue the poetic conversation.

UPDATES & BONUSES

I write a new poem every few days and love sharing inspirations and ideas with my poetry pen-friends. My monthly email will bring you my inspirational poetry news and ideas, discounted books, and other pen-friend presents. Follow the link below to become my poetry pen-friend and get a **free e-book**:

OrnaRoss.com/Free-Poetry

PLEASE REVIEW THIS BOOK ONLINE

If you enjoyed this book, please give it a quick review online by visiting the link below and selecting the "Reviews" tab. Your review doesn't have to be long or detailed. A quick star rating and a sentence or two that helps others to understand the value of this book is all that's needed. I appreciate the support more than you know. *Go raibh maith agat!*

OrnaRoss.com/Keepers

BECOME A PATRON

I reserve exclusive poems, special offers, and priority access for my patrons on Patreon. If you want monthly poetry chapbooks you can't get anywhere else, plus other books and bonuses, join me on Patreon as a poetry patron. Click the following link for more info on Patreon bonuses:

OrnaRoss.com/Poetry-Patrons

AWARD WINNING INSPIRATIONAL POETRY

Orna Ross: Inspirational Poetry Books

If you like uplifting cadences and brushes with the infinite, treat yourself to more powerful poetry
from this award-winning Irish poet.

FROM THE INSPIRATIONAL POETRY SERIES

Keepers

A book of motivational poetry that encourages you to do what you love, spurs you to greatness, picks you up when you fail and lets you know that, yes, you can make it.

"Ross's verse is technically brilliant, emotionally beguiling and, at times, startling." (Kaleem Raja, The View from Here)

To get *Keepers*, visit:
OrnaRoss.com/Keepers

Allowing Now

Covering themes like mindfulness, meditation, and self-compassion, *Allowing Now* explores the perceptions of a poet for whom everyday moments are both a treasure and an opportunity for growth.

"Not just a collection of good poetry…[but]… an exercise in wellness" (Amazon Review)

To get *Allowing Now*, visit:
OrnaRoss.com/AllowingNow

FROM THE 12 POEMS TO INSPIRE SERIES

Bright Star

An illustrated book of poems about births and beginnings. A beautiful gift for Christmas, or for anyone starting anew.

"A lovely, emotional collection, something to treasure." (*The Bookwormery*)

To get *Bright Star*, visit:
OrnaRoss.com/BrightStar

Night Light As It Rises

This illustrated, inspirational gift book explores grief, consolation, and carrying on. A thoughtful gift for hard times.

"Since my mum died I make sure to take time for honouring her and this spoke to that feeling…" (*Cozy Chapters*)

To get *Night Light as It Rises*, visit:
OrnaRoss.com/NightlightAsItRises

Circle of Life

An illustrated gift book of inspirational poems about mothering–a gift for Mother's Day, or anytime, for anyone who gives care.

To get *Circle of Life*, visit:
OrnaRoss.com/CircleOfLife

ACKNOWLEDGMENTS

My thanks to Jane Dixon-Smith for cover design of this book and the *Selected Inspirational Poetry* series. To the #IndiePoetryPlease community on Instagram, thank you for reading, thank you for writing. To the publishing team: Sarah Begley, Kayleigh Brindley and Dan Parsons, who get the words from me to the readers. To Philip Lynch, first reader and sometime muse. And a special thanks to my patrons on Patreon, who keep the poems coming. With a bow, thank you all. *Sonas libh go léir.*

x Orna

ABOUT THE POET

Orna Ross is an award-winning and bestselling novelist and poet. She writes historical fiction and inspirational poetry and is a founder-director of the Alliance of Independent Authors (ALLi). Born and raised in Wexford, in the south-east corner of Ireland, she now lives and works in London and St Leonard's-on-Sea, in the south-east corner of England.

Find out more at
OrnaRoss.com

- amazon.com/author/OrnaRoss
- goodreads.com/ornaross
- patreon.com/OrnaRoss

www.ingramcontent.com/pod-product-compliance
Lightning Source LLC
Chambersburg PA
CBHW030308100526
44590CB00012B/563